PRAYING THROUGH
THE BEATITUDES

Dan R. Crawford

7710-T Cherry Park Drive, Ste 224
Houston, TX 77095
713-766-4271
www.WorldwidePublishingGroup.com

ISBN: 978-1-68411-867-0

ENDORSEMENTS

Learning to pray Scripture is always the best way toward effective praying. Imagine praying Scripture and focusing just on the words of Jesus in Scripture and you have the power of *Praying Through The Beatitudes* by my friend Dan Crawford. Clear biblical insights, wonderful stories, and practical help combine to make this a wonderful tool to grow your prayer life.

--Dr. David Butts, Chairman, *America's National Prayer Committee*

Whether you consider yourself an expert or a novice in the area of prayer—who among us is an expert?!—Praying through the Beatitudes will broaden your knowledge and challenge your heart. Dan Crawford combines biblical explanation, current and historical examples, with daily life experiences, then he guides you to personal spiritual evaluation with convicting thought-provoking questions. The chapter, *Being Poor in Spirit*, stopped me in my tracks and led me to my knees; and that's just the first chapter. Take the time, pray through the Beatitudes, and the Lord may change your prayer life too.

--Eleanor Witcher, Prayer Office Director, *Southern Baptist International Mission Board*

This is more than a fresh look at the "beatitude" teachings of Jesus. Dr. Dan Crawford has written a guide for Christ-followers who are ready to take a reimagine-journey, to transform their perspective of prayer and practice of praying. A renewing of their mind as they are led by the Holy Spirit into scripture. Professor Crawford provides more than quality content; he presents a format that equips us to comprehend and apply the biblical teaching. He invites us to interact with the text and make application to daily life and the world around us.

Is this a book on practicing prayer or developing disciples? Yes. Both. For a new believer. For the serious student. For those leaders called to make disciples who become prayer champions.

--**Phil Miglioratti**, *Pray.Network Curator*; #ReimaginePRAYER

You can read the Beatitudes in 37 seconds (I timed it), or you can slow down, pray through them with reflections from Dan Crawford's book, and let the Spirit bring deeper meaning and application to your life. Dan crafts his narrative of the Beatitudes in a way that you can imagine Jesus sitting on the mountainside as He delivers His teaching to His disciples. The word "blessed" will take on a richer meaning as you immerse yourself in the Word, accompanied by Dan's insightful prayer guide.

--**Carol Madison**, Editor of *Prayer Connect* magazine

If you are hungry for a teaching menu of meat—rather than milk—on Jesus Christ's opening "Blessed are..." declarations in His "Sermon on The Mount", Dr. Dan Crawford's workbook will more than satisfy your appetite! Not just for its biblical insight, but also for its personal application in focusing your prayer life on praying "in agreement" with God's Word!

--**Dennis Conner**, Prayer Coach with Called to Serve Prayer Ministry, Inc.

I get excited when I see another book by Dr. Dan Crawford, because I know it will not only be good; but also, it will teach me something for my walk with the Lord. His new book, *Praying through the Beatitudes,* does not disappoint! Between Dr. Dan's clear word definitions, heartwarming stories, and classic, related quotes, you will come away from reading this book inspired and fully equipped to pray through the beatitudes for yourself and others. I am giving this a try and I hope you will too.

Dr. Dan Crawford's presentation of *Praying Through the Beatitudes*, is the best put together, insightful and useful presentation of The Beatitudes that I have ever read. It is scholastically solid, biblically-based, filled with clear and powerful illustrations and easily useful as a workbook for personal or group study. It is just simply enjoyable to read! Anyone will be richly blessed and grow spiritually if they choose to make this delightful journey of *Praying Through the Beatitudes.*

Dr. Dan has a secret to tell, a mystery to unravel: How to achieve an ultimate inward distinctive bliss untouchable by life. It's been hidden in plain sight for centuries, but no longer. In this simple interactive book, the way to achieving a blessed life is revealed. Now, the only question is: How much do you want it?

Contents

Dedication

To my faithful prayer partners.

You know who you are.

And to the memory of my younger brother, "Breakfast" Bob Crawford, who "blessed" the lives of all with whom he came in contact.

PREFACE

I saw him sitting on a couch reading a Bible. It was early morning at the mall near my home, and I was walking with other senior adults. He was by far the youngest person in the yet-to-be-opened mall. As I circled around him a couple of times, I developed a profile – Seminary student who dropped off his wife at the mall where she worked, and he was passing time before his first class of the morning. This was a logical profile, since the seminary was nearby and many a student owned only one vehicle between him and his wife.

As a retired Seminary professor, I figured we'd have something to talk about, so, I sat down next to him and asked, "What are you reading?" His reply was, "I'm reading the *be-a-tudes*" with emphasis on the "be." This was my first clue that he might not be a seminary student, since even a first semester student would know how to pronounce "beatitudes.

Pressing on, I asked, "Are you a Seminary student?" "No!" he replied, "I'm homeless."

I was a bit thrown off with this answer, but we continued our conversation. Long story short – I got him a job busing tables at a local restaurant with a manager friend, but it only lasted a few weeks, and he disappeared.

Meanwhile I prayed for him, and since I knew he was actually referring to the beatitudes, and since the beatitudes had always been special to me, I actually prayed through the beatitudes for him.

Another reason the beatitudes are special to me stems from an event in 1998. My wife and I were on a tour of the Holy Land with my faculty colleague, Dr. Bill Tolar, who introduced us to Sam Philipe, a famous Israeli sculptor. While he is famous for his "Jerusalem Globe" (which I purchased), my wife secretly purchased his sculpture of Jesus delivering his Sermon on the Mount, with the beatitudes engraved on a plaque under the sculpture. This sculpture later became a gift on a special occasion. I have treasured it through the years, displaying on a prominent place in my office.

Wikipedia has the following information about Sam Philipe:

Shlomo (Sam) Philipe was born in Jerusalem to an old Jerusalem family. A fifth-generation Jerusalmite, he started his artistic career while serving as a paramedic with the Israel Defense Forces as a combat medic, he spent a year in New York City restoring antique furniture and studying art. When he returned to Israel in 1989, he opened a studio in Jerusalem. Philipe's sculptures have been presented to government leaders around the world as gifts from the Israeli government. Outdoor sculptures by Philipe have been installed at various locations in Jerusalem, while many of his smaller sculptures, crafted from sterling silver and 24 karat gold, are mounted on polished stone bases using stones from the desert. Philipe often uses blocks of Jerusalem stone or black basalt from the Galilee as pedestals for his work. Philipe's goal was to "reach God through art." He created sculptures based on Bible themes in the belief that his work transports viewers back to ancient times and allows them to feel a connection to the Bible in their own life.

We were blessed to have our picture taken with him as he worked.

Now out of print is a book I wrote, entitled, *DiscipleShape: Twelve Weeks to Spiritual Fitness*, in which I began with the beatitudes, as a training guide for spiritual fitness. This book is an adaptation of the first three chapters of that book, with prayer pointers added. In each section designed for prayer, I have shared one prayer to get you started, then left three other spaces for your prayers. It is my hope that He will guide you in praying through the beatitudes, either for yourself or for others.

Praying scripture is not new. In fact, it is biblical. Both Jonah, in the belly of a great fish, and Jesus, on a cross, prayed from the Psalms. In his book, *Psalms: The Prayer Book of the Bible*, the German martyr Dietrich Bonhoeffer reminds us that when we pray Scripture, we are praying with Jesus:

> All prayers of the Bible are such prayers which we pray together with Jesus Christ, in which he accompanies us, and through which he brings us into the presence of God. Otherwise there are no true prayers, for only in and with Jesus Christ can we truly pray. If we want to read and to pray the prayers of the Bible and especially the Psalms, therefore, we must not ask first what they have to do with us, but what they have to do with Jesus Christ.

In *God's Prayer Book*, Ben Patterson recommends the three Rs, as a means by which we can pray the scriptures: *Rejoice, Repent, Request*. I add to these, four additional Rs: *Reflect* (an exegesis of the beatitude), *Reward* (a consideration of the promise made in each beatitude), *Review* (to simply help the reader personalize the beatitude), and *Request for Others* (which is another way of saying intercession, since the majority of the prayers in the Bible are intercessory in nature. We will use these to guide our praying.

So, pray along with me as we explore the beatitudes of Jesus.

Dr. Dan R. Crawford, Senior Professor, Evangelism & Missions, Chair of Prayer Emeritus, *Southwestern Baptist Theological Seminary*

Fort Worth, Texas 76133

INTRODUCTION

The mighty Mississippi River winds 2,350 miles from its beginning near the U.S.--Canada border to its ending at the Gulf of Mexico. In comparing its size and majesty to other rivers they knew, the Native Americans named it the "great river." More than a mile in width in some places, it digs to a bed of 100 feet in other places. With more than 250 tributaries, the Mississippi is one of the longest river systems in the world. As great as the Mississippi River is, it all begins as a two-foot deep, narrow stream, flowing out of Lake Itasca in north central Minnesota.

Likewise, the volumes that have been written about the Sermon on the Mount begin in these eight statements of Jesus called beatitudes.

The beatitudes of Jesus have also been called attributes, a more descriptive term. The word beatitude is a name derived from Latin, a rough translation of *beatus*, referring to a state of happiness or bliss. Attributes are defined as inherent characteristics. They are often used for identification purposes in a painting or a sculpture. In scripture Jesus repeatedly (eight times in all) draws attention to some aspect of the character of the person who would follow him.

When you are born into a family, you inherit certain characteristics of that family. Likewise, when you enter the family of God, you become known by certain inherent characteristics or attributes. Jesus says his disciples are known by these inherent attributes or beatitudes.

The Sermon on the Mount, of which these first twelve verses are a part, has been called the essence of the Christian life, the central document of the Christian faith, Christianity 101, Earth's Greatest Sermon, God's Magna Charta, A Pattern for Life, Christ's Inaugural Address, The Keys to the Kingdom, The Manifesto of the Kingdom, and many other eloquent descriptions. While this sermon contains ideas far ahead even of our advanced time, to the instructor and the instructed, it is basic and fundamental. It begins, as Jesus began with his first disciples, with a look at spiritual attributes.

"And when He saw the multitudes." Jesus always saw people in the light of what they could become rather than in their present state. Like the drill instructor looking at raw recruits and seeing beyond their present condition to what they would become in weeks of intensive training, so Jesus saw more in this crowd than anyone else. So, it is with us. Jesus looks beyond our pain to our possibilities, beyond the hazards to the hope, beyond the mire to the meaning, and sees what we can become.

But, before beginning to speak, Jesus *"went up on the mountain."* Since Jesus was still in Galilee this could have been any of the many hills above the sea, yet the mountain does not dominate the message, the location does not dictate the lesson, the site is not paramount over the sermon.

There Jesus *"sat down"* to teach his disciples. Often Jewish rabbis would teach their students while walking in the countryside or in the city streets. However, when official teaching was to be shared, it was always done from a seated position. Thus, synagogue sermons were delivered while seated (Luke 4:20). The fact that Jesus sat down underlines the significance of his teaching. No casual teaching was this, but crucial, strategic, official teaching.

Interestingly enough, when Jesus sat down, his disciples *"came to Him."* One of the major characteristics of Jesus was his approachability. No one ever needed to feel as though they could not or should not approach Jesus. Thus, these unfit, spiritually out of shape, poorly equipped disciples *"came to Him."*

Then *"He opened His mouth and He began to teach them."* Having prayed all night the night before, Jesus was now ready. Thus, begins the beatitudes, with the word, *"blessed."*

BLESSED

A rumor had spread among the people that Jesus was returning to Galilee. It was whispered from small group to small group, from home to home, and business to business. Excitement grew. Suddenly, Jesus arrived, followed by his newly- called disciples and a multitude from Decapolis, Jerusalem, Judea, and beyond Jordan. Others from Tiberius, Bethsaida, and Capernaum would soon join them.

Together these new followers fell in line, leaving their places of business, their homes, their places of learning, their leisure activities. They followed him until they reached the summit of a dusty hill. There Jesus motioned for them to sit. Overwhelming anxiety gripped the multitude as they waited expectantly. His first word to them was *"blessed,"* the Greek word being *markarios,* which is a complete, self-contained joy. Some, feeling the translation *"blessed"* to be too religious, have substituted the word, happy, but this translation is entirely too secular.

Happiness is a chief goal of humankind. Many philosophers have held that happiness is the *summon bonum*—the highest good in life. In writing the Declaration of Independence, Thomas Jefferson wrote about the "right to life, liberty, and the pursuit of happiness." This pursuit has caused humankind to look in many places and try numerous experiences to discover happiness.

One French philosopher said, "The whole world is on a mad quest for security and happiness." This quest has led to interesting pursuits. It was said that Leo Tolstoy, the Russian fiction writer and social reformer, was told by his older brother Nicholas that the secret of happiness is for everybody to love everybody else and the rules for such a life were written on a green stick buried in the forest under an oak tree near a deep, dark ravine. Ernest Newton in his book entitled, *This Book- Collecting Game*, states about one of his characters, "Gilbert White discovered the formula for complete happiness, but died before making the announcement." A book of famous quotations lists 137 quotes on the subject of happiness. The quest for happiness is universal, but for many happiness is elusive.

Happiness has within it the seeds of its own disqualification. The word is based on hap – a chance, a happenstance, whereas the kind of happiness referred to by Jesus means more than this. This "man of sorrows" knew the real meaning of happiness was based not on probabilities, but upon certainties.

Nor is the word *"blessed"* enough when judged by the popular use of the word. We tend to relate blessing to the material things of life, but this falls far short of the meaning as used by Jesus. This word *markarios* here refers more to an inward, distinctive joy and bliss. It is an inner joy that is untouched by the things of this world and unrelated to the outward accumulation of possessions.

The full meaning of *markarios* may perhaps best be understood when seen from the perspective of the Greeks themselves. They called the island of Cyprus, *hemarkia* (the feminine form of *markarios*) which literally meant The Happy Isle. So beautiful, lovely, rich, and fertile was Cyprus that the Greeks believed a person would never need to leave its shores to find genuine happiness. The climate, flowers, fruits, trees, minerals, and natural resources on Cyprus were everything anyone required. Thus, *markarios* describes a distinctive joy whose secret is within itself, untouchable, self-contained, independent of all the happenings of life.

This blessedness was superior to the blessedness known by persons in the past. Just as the Ten Commandments of the Old Testament summarize the Law, so these eight attributes of the New Testament summarize the gospel. Moses was a servant of God; Jesus was the Son of God. Moses came down from a mountain with ten statements engraved on stone tablets. Jesus spoke from a mountain eight statements that became engraved on human hearts and minds. Moses spoke of the law, judgment, and wrath. Jesus opened his mouth and said, *"Blessed."* The laws spoken by Moses related to outward conduct. The attributes spoken by Jesus related to an inward attitude. Moses spoke of the kind of life one must live to be godly. Jesus spoke of the blessedness of those who are godly. In contrast to the old words stands this new word: "*blessed.*"

Likewise, this blessedness is superior to the blessedness known in the present world. Over against the worlds offer of quick-fix solutions is this word "*blessed.*" Over against the world's offer of delight through dependencies is this word "*blessed.*" Over against the worlds offer of meaning through madness is the word "*blessed.*" Today the world's beatitudes might read like this:

Blessed are the movers and shakers, for they get what they want

in this world.

Blessed are those who insulate themselves with a hard shell, for

they never get hurt by life.

Blessed are those who gripe and complain, for they seem to get

all the attention.

Blessed are the apathetic, for they never feel another's pain.

Blessed are the workaholics, for they get results and promotions.

Blessed are they that explore outer space, for they shall fill the

inner void.

Blessed are they who place all their faith in hi-tech, for the

future belongs to them.

Blessed are the intellectuals, for they know how to cope with

life.

Blessed are the religious, for they will know inner peace.

Finally, this blessedness is superior to what the world offers for the future. Today's voices loudly and confidently proclaim their promises of future hope: utopia reached through universalism, an eternity of eradication, an inheritance of annihilation, a future based on fatalism. If you give today, God will bless you tomorrow, proclaims a televangelist. Others have named it the delayed gratification ethic. Contrast these offers to the words of Jesus concerning the future of His disciples. Using the same word, *markarios*, Jesus speaks from heaven saying, "Blessed are the dead who die in the Lord . . . that they may rest from their labors" (Revelation 14:13).

Having pronounced his disciples "*blessed,*" Jesus begins to list attributes or characteristics often called beatitudes. Eight times Jesus draws attention to an inherent characteristic of one who could be called truly blessed and in so doing outlines the attributes of a disciple.

Keeping in mind the meaning of *markarios*, what would have to happen today for you to feel genuinely blessed? Spend some time in prayer right now. Ask God to help you feel blessed today.

CHAPTER ONE: BEING POOR IN SPIRIT

REFLECT

" *B*lessed are the poor in spirit" (Matthew 5:3). When Jesus spoke about being poor, he received the undivided attention of many who had come to listen that day. Few things get our attention and response faster than an empty wallet. Yet the poverty of which Jesus spoke was of the spirit. If we are honest with ourselves, we often go days, weeks, months, maybe even years with an empty heart. We are poor in spirit. For me, parts of my seminary education were like this. I would sometimes find myself so caught up in academics that I lost touch with devotion. I knew how to exegete scripture, but I didn't know how to exercise spirituality. It doesn't have to be either/or. It ought to be both/and. But for me, I was studying with an empty heart, spiritually bankrupt.

This particular beatitude calls for a complete re-evaluation of true wealth. Surely, wealth is not achieved with the possession of things. Paul said of Jesus, "Though He was rich, yet for your sake He became poor, that you through His poverty might become rich" (2 Corinthians 8:9). Concerning himself, Paul wrote:

> Whatever things were gain to me, those things I have counted as loss for the sake of Christ. More than that, I count all things to be loss in view of the surpassing value of knowing Christ Jesus my Lord, for whom I have suffered the loss of all things, and count them but rubbish so that I may gain Christ. (Philippians 3:7-8)

Those things that have constituted wealth and likewise those things that have constituted poverty must be re-evaluated in-light of this beatitude. For those of us who live in an affluent society, this is a difficult idea for us to grasp. We have become victims of our environment.

The Danish philosopher and theologian, Soren Kierkegaard, told of observing a group of wild ducks as they flew during migration time. They landed briefly on a farm pond where a farmer was distributing corn for his tame ducks. When they flew on, one duck decided to stay and enjoy the corn. When time came for the ducks to fly back to the south, this lone duck tried to join them, only to discover his wings would no longer allow him to leave the ground. He had become a victim of his environment. It is easy for us to be like the lone duck.

In fact, poverty in our day may be best described in this poem by Debbie Groves:

Poverty is having many acquaintances and not knowing any of them.

Poverty is having so many clothes that you —haven't a thing to wear.

Poverty is eating so well you have to think about going on a diet.

Poverty is having every pill imaginable to cure your body's ills because you can't afford to be sick.

Poverty is parents who keep their marriage together for your sake.

Poverty is being loaded down with toys at birthdays and Christmas and Then being bored silly because there's nothing to do.

Poverty is having two cars, three TVs, and a dishwasher and then roughing it‖ by going camping to get away from it all.

Poverty is the day-to-day going from one building to the next and never stopping to see the beauty in the world outside.

Poverty is spending money on makeup, deodorants, talcs, and colognes, and still being worried about the image you are projecting.

Poverty is never being curious about the world around you, never wanting to explore it or the people in it.

Poverty is of the soul as well as the body.

To be poor in spirit is to recognize our spiritual poverty apart from God, to declare spiritual bankruptcy, to realize our own inadequacy. It is to rearrange our résumé, emphasizing those attributes that are from God over those accomplishments that are from self. We may have houses and land and possessions of many kinds, but as a spiritually fit disciple we will possess these things without allowing them to possess us. Indeed, the realization and admission that we are a no one, allows you to meet The One who can make you a someone. As a young, inexperienced preacher, I stood one Sunday with my well prepared yet prayer-less sermon, and began to deliver it in my own spiritually unfit strength. Early in this futile attempt to communicate I remember thinking of the words to an old hymn by Augustus M. Toplady:

Nothing in my hands I bring

Simply to thy cross I cling;

Naked, come to thee for dress;

Helpless, look to thee for grace;

Foul, I to the fountain fly;

Wash me, Savior, or I die!

How then can we become poor in spirit? First, recognize our own spiritual poverty. Admit that we have no hits in twenty times at bat. Someone has said, "No man is so ignorant as he who knows nothing and knows not that he knows nothing. No man is so sick as he who has a fatal disease and is not aware of it. No man is so poor as he who is destitute and yet thinks he is rich."

Jesus told of a rich man who miscalculated his wealth:

I will say to my soul, "Soul, you have many goods laid up for many

Years to come; take your ease, eat, drink and be merry." But God said to

him, "You fool! This very night your soul is required of you; and now

who will own what you have prepared?" So is the man who lays up

treasure for himself and is not rich toward God. (Luke 12:19-21)

In God's economy helplessness leads to power, emptiness leads to filling, confession leads to freedom, dependence leads to independence, and poverty leads to wealth.

Second, see all gifts, graces, and benefits as being from God. Acknowledge that you scored a basket only because a teammate fed you the ball. The word used by Jesus in this attribute is *ptochos* and means a beggar who lives off the alms of another. The same word described the beggar Lazarus in the parable told by Jesus in Luke 16:20. Like King David, we must acknowledge, "All things come from You" (1. Chronicles 29:14), and like Job we must declare, "Naked I came from my mother's womb, and naked I shall return there. The Lord gave and the Lord has taken away. Blessed be the name of the Lord" (Job 1:21).

Third, take no false pride in accomplishments, achievements, or awards. Affirm that you won the race because God gave you the ability to run. The opposite of poor in spirit is proud in spirit. The story is told of a woodpecker who took great pride in the fact that while he was pecking on a tree, lightning struck and split the tree in half. And then there is the story of the ant and the elephant who walked dangerously over a hanging bridge. The bridge shook and squeaked and quaked but did not break. On the other side the ant commented, "Man, did we shake that bridge!" These are examples of false pride. James says, "God is opposed to the proud, but gives grace to the humble" (James 4:6).

Fourth, compare yourself to no one but Jesus Christ. Announce that your Most Valuable Player trophy looks small compared to a cross. Satan's strategy causes us to compare ourselves to others, especially those who are weaker. Whatever we are today, someone will be greater tomorrow; and whatever we accomplish today, someone will accomplish more tomorrow. Napoleon captured this earthly comparison with one statement: "I am doing now what will fill thousands of volumes in this generation. In the next, one volume will contain it all. In the third, a paragraph, and in the fourth, a single line." Comparison is only valid when we compare ourselves to our Lord. This comparison reminds us of our spiritual poverty.

Fifth, exercise spiritual muscle. Activate the abilities God has given you. In my early years of ministry an older minister counseled me, "Don't ever refuse an opportunity to speak for Jesus Christ." I've tried to the best of my time and health to follow his advice. The more you serve, the more you're reminded of spiritual poverty and total dependence on Jesus. C. H. Spurgeon said, "The way to rise in the kingdom is to sink in ourselves." John the Baptist said of Jesus, "He must increase, but I must decrease" (John 3:30).

REWARD

Each beatitude is followed by a promise, a reward for those who live-up to the beatitude. Each reward has an earthly and a heavenly application. For those who are poor in spirit, Jesus responded, *"theirs is the kingdom of heaven"* (Matthew 5:3). This phrase is a favorite of Matthew (appearing thirty-two times in his gospel account) and corresponds to the phrases "the kingdom" and "the kingdom of God" used by other gospel writers. It is a reference to part of a society where God's will is done on earth, even as in heaven.

This kingdom is both here and now as well as then and there. We who profess faith in Christ have dual citizenship. I am a citizen of the United States because I was born here. I am a citizen of heaven because I have been reborn. The phrase refers to a reign more than a region, to a presence more than a place and belongs uniquely to the followers of Jesus Christ. The full meaning of the word "theirs" is "theirs and theirs alone."

What a tragedy to be a follower of Jesus, an heir of the kingdom, and not understand its present reality in our hearts. Graham Kendrick captured this present tense kingdom with his words:

The kingdom of our God is here. Heaven is in my heart.

The presence of His majesty. Heaven is in my heart.

And in His presence joy abounds. Heaven is in my heart.

The light of holiness surrounds. Heaven in my heart.

There was something different about Morris Siegel. On the surface he seemed like an average Los Angeles street person -- roaming about in dark alleys, sleeping outdoors, carrying all he owned in an old shopping cart. He died the way one expects a street person to die -- in an alley. But something about him was different. Maybe it was his three bank accounts containing a total of $207,421.

Ten years earlier, Morris' father had died and left the money to him. When Morris did not claim it, the Division of Unclaimed Property tracked him down, and his family forced him to accept it. He did not show up at the ceremony when the cash was handed over. He took enough of the money to buy an old car, where he slept in bad weather. Relatives rented an apartment for him, but he never went there. He died December 14, 1989, with three dollars in his pocket and an untouched fortune in the bank.

Old Morris lived a wasted life and died a futile death, but we can't be too quick to point a finger at him. He was only dealing with the temporary while many of us are playing the same losing game with the eternal.

Finally, we can pray with Hannah, "The Lord makes poor and rich; He brings low, He also exalts. He raises the poor from the dust, He lifts the needy from the ash heap to make them sit with nobles" (1 Samuel 2:7-8). Those who come to God in spiritual poverty, with broken hearts, depart with spiritual wealth and mended hearts: "For thus says the high and exalted One who lives forever, whose name is Holy. I dwell on a high and holy place, and also with the contrite and lowly of spirit in order to revive the spirit of the lowly and to revive the heart of the contrite" (Isaiah 57:15). When in admission of spiritual poverty we give up our own little kingdoms, God replaces them with the kingdom of heaven.

REVIEW

"To be poor in spirit . . . is to rearrange your résumé." Think about your résumé and how you want to be known. What are the priority characteristics on your résumé? Does "poor in spirit" appear? How could it be a part of your résumé?

1. Lord, give me a greater desire to be "poor in spirit"?

2._____

_____

_____

3._____

_____

_____

4._____

_____

_____

REJOICE

1. Thank You, Lord that being "poor in spirit" has little to do with earthly financial status or the lack thereof.

2._____

_____

_____

3._____

_____

_____

4._____

_____

_____

REPENT

1. Forgive me Lord for seeking earthly gain and accomplishment in to earn status in Your Kingdom, for being possessed by my possessions.

2._____

_____

_____

3._____

_____

_____

4._____

_____

_____

REQUEST FOR SELF

1. Out of my spiritual poverty, Lord, help me to view what You give me as stewardship, not ownership.

2._____

_____

_____

3._____

_____

_____

4._____

_____

_____

REQUEST FOR OTHERS

1. All that I have Lord, has been given to me so that I might share it with others. Because their needs are great, today, I pray for

_____

2._____

_____

_____

3._____

_____

_____

4._____

_____

_____

CHAPTER TWO: BEING MOURNFUL

REFLECT

"*Blessed are those who mourn*" (Matthew 5:4). Sorrow is described by nine different words in the New Testament, but the strongest of these words, *pantheo,* is used here. It refers to a grief so consuming that it cannot be hidden. The same word is used to describe the reaction of the disciples following the death of Jesus. When Mary Magdalene rushed to inform them of the resurrection, she found them "mourning and weeping" (Mark 16:10).

It seems strange to speak of the blessedness of the brokenhearted, the joy of sorrow, the gladness of grief, the treasure of tears. If you are blessed, why would you mourn? If you mourned, how could you be blessed? But this is God's plan and from it we learn not only how to cope with life's sorrows but also how to know and understand God better.

There is a story about a Jewish rabbi who was deeply loved by his students. One day an outgoing student rushed into the rabbi's office and exclaimed, "Do you know I love you?" The rabbi looked up from his books and asked, "Do you know what hurts me?" Confused, the student responded, "Your question is irrelevant." "No," returned the rabbi. "Only if you know what hurts me, can you really love me."

Through our mourning, we enter into a deeper understanding of the "man of sorrows" who was "acquainted with grief" (Isaiah 53:3), and having learned from him, we can then bear our own sorrows. Robert Browning Hamilton wrote:

I walked a mile with Pleasure.

She chattered all the way,

But left me none the wiser

For all she had to say.

I walked a mile with Sorrow.

And ne'er a word said she;

But, oh, the things I learned from her,

When Sorrow walked with me!

There are three general areas in which we mourn: for human sorrows, for the evils of this world, and for the sin in our own lives. First, we mourn over human sorrow. Mourning occurs in those who have lost teenagers to peer pressure, a spouse to another love or to death, a job to someone more qualified, a home to fire, flood, or storm, a degree to financial or academic shortcomings, or an exercise program to an injury. The mourning takes place whether the reasons are justified or not.

Some mourning over human disappointment is needed. The musician Elgar heard a beautiful young girl give an almost flawless performance and then responded, "She will be great when something happens to break her heart."

Some mourning is so private we are prone to sing the words of the old Spiritual, "Nobody knows the trouble I've seen." Paul wrote to young Timothy concerning an unknown sorrow: "I constantly remember you in my prayers night and day, longing to see you, even as I recall your tears" (2 Timothy 1:3-4).

Perhaps the greatest of human sorrows is the mourning related to death. Following his wife's death, Abraham "went in to mourn for Sarah and to weep for her" (Genesis 23:2). The shortest verse in the Bible expresses the mourning of Jesus at the death of Lazarus: "Jesus wept" (John 11:35).

A woman in a church where I served as Interim Pastor lost her mother unexpectedly on a Friday following routine surgery. I conducted the funeral on Sunday afternoon. On Tuesday the woman's father died, and his funeral was held on Thursday. In six days, she lost both parents. Apart from the comfort that is promised to those who mourn, she could not have borne this sorrow. In Hamlet, Shakespeare writes, "When sorrows come, they come not as single spies, but in battalions."

The Irish poet Thomas Moore, overwhelmed by the death of his oldest daughter, followed by the death of his youngest daughter wrote:

Come, ye disconsolate, where're ye languish,

Come to the mercy seat, fervently kneel,

Here bring your wounded hearts, here tell your anguish;

Earth has no sorrow that heav'n cannot heal.

A second area of life where we often mourn is in our relationship to the evils of this world: children of addicted parents, women abused, mental institutions, AIDS victims and their families, terminal cancer, divorce courts. While there are often innocent victims in each of these cases, we mourn the consequences of the evil that effects them. Abraham Lincoln said, "I feel sorry for the man who can't feel the whip when it is laid on the other man's back."

The captive children of Israel did not adapt to the conditions of Babylon and the injustices experienced there, but rather mourned for the return and restoration of Jerusalem. That which the world offers often leaves us in sorrow.

When Jesus thought of Jerusalem he lamented, "O Jerusalem, Jerusalem, who kills the prophets and stones those who are sent to her! How often I wanted to gather your children together, the way a hen gathers her chicks under her wings, and you were unwilling" (Matthew 23:37).

I have a pastor friend who drove to the top of a high hill over the city in which he served. As he thought of his city and the many injustices of it, he wept. He said he went there to pray but was overcome with the thoughts of evil in his city. His thoughts that day could have matched those of Frank Laubach who said, "Forgive me Lord for ever looking on my world with dry eyes."

The Greek word mourn was translated by Martin Luther into the German word *leidtragen,* meaning sorrow-bearing. Recently a drive-by shooting happened near my office. An eleven-year-old girl was accidentally killed by a bullet meant for another. While the little girl's mother was shown weeping, the television stations repeatedly aired a tape of a neighbor of the deceased, crying and asking why. She was "sorrow-bearing" for a fellow mother.

Still a third area in which we mourn is the area of sin in our lives. This is most likely the mourning Jesus had first in mind when he stated this beatitude. It is here that the Christian life begins. Just as physical pain precedes physical birth so mourning over sin precedes spiritual birth. Just as conviction of sin must precede salvation, so you must grieve over your sin before asking Jesus to forgive you. As we continue to sin, we continue to mourn over our sin. Just as sore muscles precede physical fitness, so confession precedes forgiveness and spiritual fitness. Yet how much better to mourn for sin and ask forgiveness than mourn because of the consequences of unforgiven sin.

Sin continues to pervade our life even though we have been saved. We continue to be tempted and we continue to yield to temptation. The closer we live with the Lord, the more we are conscious of our own sin. Isaiah became keenly aware of his sin when he came into the presence of God (Isaiah 6:5). Standing unworthy in the presence of a holy God, standing unholy on holy ground, standing with unclean lips in the presence of holy perfection, Isaiah cried out with a mixture of confession and adoration.

One of the interesting studies in the life of Paul is how he viewed himself as his knowledge of Jesus increased. Around A.D. 48, Paul described himself as "an apostle (not sent from men nor through the agency of man, but through Jesus Christ and God the Father, who raised Him from the dead)" (Galatians 1:1). Around A.D. 55 Paul described himself as "the least of the apostles" (1 Corinthians 15:9). In A.D. 63, Paul called himself "the very least of all saints" (Ephesians 3:8). And finally, after years of missionary labor and years of walking with his Lord,

Paul identified himself by saying, "Jesus came into the world to save sinners, among whom I am foremost of all" (1 Timothy 1:15).

The more we walk with and know the Lord, the more we are likely to mourn over our own sins. The 18th century missionary to the American Indians, David Brainerd, wrote in his journal on October 18, 1740, "In my morning devotions my soul was exceedingly melted and bitterly mourned over my exceeding sinfulness and vileness."

REWARD

Following this beatitude of mourning is the resulting reward, *"they shall be comforted"* (Matthew 5:4). The word for comforted is *parakalein* and it has four meanings. The first is the obvious idea of comfort, yet this is the rarest meaning. The second is helper or counselor. When Jesus told his disciples he was going away, he promised to send them "another Helper" (John 14:16), a reference to the Holy Spirit. The third meaning is encouragement or exhortation, that is, a challenge to get back in the midst of life having been temporarily sidetracked by sorrow.

Finally, the word comforted includes the idea of being invited to a banquet or celebration. Jesus said, "Blessed are you who weep now, for you shall laugh" (Luke 6:21). The Psalmist promised, "Those who sow in tears shall reap with joyful shouting" (Psalm 126:5) and "Weeping may last for the night, but a shout of joy comes in the morning" (Psalm 30:5). How many times have we seen the teammates of an injured athlete mourning over an injury? Then the same team, dedicates the game or the season to the injured colleague and eventually we are treated to the scene of a victorious locker room where someone reminds the world that they won for their fallen teammate. The grief had given way to celebration.

It is sometimes difficult to understand how mourning could result in comfort. There is a story of a German castle, where a man strung wires from tower to tower to make a giant wind harp. However, he completed the task in the summer when there was no wind. People wondered how the wire was going to create music. The autumn winds brought some sounds, but not enough to satisfy those who looked on in wonder.

However, when the violent storms of winter arrived, they brought a full symphony. As real musical sounds came with the cold, uncomfortable winter, so God blesses our sorrow with comfort.

This much we know: whatever mourning exists in this life and to whatever degree our Lord comforts and relieves that mourning, it will someday end. In John's picture of heaven he says, "He will wipe away every tear from their eyes; and there will no longer be any death; there will no longer be any mourning, or crying, or pain" (Revelation 21:4).

REVIEW

Keeping in mind the meaning of *pantheo,* how long has it been since you mourned? What is one sin in your life over which you mourn? Commit it to God in prayer.

1. Lord, I commit this one sin (surely there are others, but let's begin with one) to You right now, so that I may mourn correctly over it.

2._____

_____

_____

3._____

_____

_____

4._____

_____

_____

REJOICE

1. Thank You, Lord, for the ability to care, for if we did not care, we would not mourn.

2._____

_____

_____

3._____

_____

_____

4._____

_____

_____

REPENT

1. Forgive me Lord for not caring enough to mourn as I ought.

2._____

_____

_____

3._____

_____

_____

4._____

_____

_____

REQUEST FOR SELF

1. Lord, I confess that I am afraid of Your comfort, because it implies

that I need comforting, and I'd rather not need to be comforted, but help me to understand the true meaning of Your comfort, so I can gladly accept it.

2._____

_____

_____

3._____

_____

_____

4._____

_____

_____

REQUEST FOR OTHERS

1. Lord, as I learn how to mourn properly, may I be of comfort to my friend _____.

2._____

_____

_____

3._____

_____

_____

4._____

_____

_____

CHAPTER THREE: BEING MEEK

REFLECT

"*Blessed are the meek*" (Matthew 5:5, KJV). The word translated by some as "meek" and others as "gentle" is *praus*. But this word does not mean today what it meant when Jesus uttered it. The idea of weak, soft, or mild is not at all the proper meaning. Given that meaning, what meek person ever inherited the earth? The Romans sought power and despised meekness. The Jews were looking for a military messiah. No one in Jesus' day had a category to describe meekness. It is the same in our day. Ask someone, "Who inherits the earth?" and names of powerful persons or countries come to mind as do board rooms and power politics. We are a people of power and might. No one has ever really lived in Mr. Rogers' Neighborhood.

In 1675 Sir Christopher Wren, the architect, laid the cornerstone for St. Paul's Cathedral in London after thirty-five years of construction. In 1710 Queen Anne paid a visit to the Cathedral. Wren waited anxiously for her reaction. Completing her tour, the Queen remarked, "It is awful, it is amusing, and it is artificial." The great architect breathed a sigh of relief. In 1710 awful meant awe-inspiring, amusing meant amazing, and artificial meant artistic. Words change in meaning. Such is the case with *praus*.

The word used by Jesus, meant focusing on the needs of others rather than on the needs of self. Others' needs are of more importance than the things we possess or the ideas we defend or the achievements we accomplish. As others' needs become elevated, personal needs become relegated. Also, the one who is meek focuses on persons rather than things. Cultivating relationships is more important than collecting things. The status in life for a disciple is measured by the character of acquaintances rather than the amount of possessions.

Likewise, the one who is meek focuses on love rather than revenge. There is a story of an elderly minister who was awakened one morning to the sound of the tiles being torn off his roof and thrown to the ground by some of his enemies. He awakened his wife with instructions to fix a big breakfast. Inviting his enemies into the house, he insisted they eat since they had been working so hard. Prior to eating, the old minister prayed for his enemies and their families. Following breakfast, they went out and put the tiles back on the roof—a response to meekness when revenge was possible.

Often words are best understood when they become flesh. Two persons in the Bible are referred to as meek. One person is Moses who was anything but weak. Contrast this man who stands without his sandals before a burning bush in humility, submission, gentleness, tameness and patience with the man who confronted the mightiest ruler of his day with these words, "Thus says the Lord, the God of Israel, Let My people go!" (Exodus 5:1). It is the same man, Moses, of whom it was written, "Now the man Moses was very meek, above all the men which were upon the face of the earth" (Numbers 12:3 (KJV).

Jesus is the second person called meek in the Bible. Contrast this man who came into Jerusalem "meek, and sitting upon an ass [donkey]" (Matthew 21:5 KJV) with the man who twice drove the money changers out of the Temple and overthrew their tables (John 2:13-16; Luke 19:45-48). It is the same man, Jesus, who on one occasion said, "Take my yoke upon you, and learn of me; for I am meek and lowly in heart" (Matthew 11:29 KJV).

This contrast is further seen in the following poem by Harry Kemp:

I saw the Conquerors riding by

With cruel lips and faces wan:

Musing on kingdoms sacked and burned

There rode the Mongol Genghis Kahn;

And Alexander, like a god,

Who sought to weld the world in one;

And Caesar with his laurel wreath;

And like the thing from Hell, the Hun;

And leading, like a star the van,

Heedless of upstretched arm and groan

Inscrutable Napoleon went,

Dreaming of empire, and alone.

Then all they perished from the earth

As fleeting shadows from a glass

And, conquering down the centuries,

Came Christ, the Swordless, on an ass!

There are essentially five meanings of the word meek. First, it means gentleness. The world says, "might is right," "dog eat dog," and "the survival of the fittest." These secular philosophies are glamorized by movies, magazines and the media. In contrast, the disciple acts in gentleness even when he or she has the ability to act with severity.

Second, it means submissiveness. Again, the world says, "be in control," "wear clothes that show power," and "use hairstyles and makeup that demonstrate authority." In contrast, the disciple stands empty-handed before God in total dependence and self-surrender.

Third, it means tameness, coming from the idea of breaking the will of a wild animal so it can be used more efficiently. It is strength under control. The world says "go wild," "live it up," and "party hearty." In contrast, the disciple allows God to break their sinful, selfish will and remake them into what they could never have been before. It causes man to disallow anyone to own him. He is not for sale, but has surrendered himself to a higher cause.

Fourth, it means patience. The world says, "now," demonstrated by its quick-fix, fast food, instant copies, minute-lube, while-you-wait attitude. In contrast, the disciple is "quick to hear, slow to speak and slow to anger" (James 1:19).

Fifth, it means humility. The world says, "I've earned my keep," "What's mine is mine," and "I deserve more." In contrast, the disciple understands that everything is a gift from God, based on grace.

These five meanings of the word meek are personified in the life of George Frederick Handel. In his later days this stooped-shouldered old man could be seen shuffling through the dark streets of London. When his music was performed, the four decades of thrilling work was often broken up by street gangs. His small fortune was gradually depleted resulting in abject poverty. His health was broken, and he was paralyzed on his right side. The medical doctors gave him no hope. But he worked, took hot baths for hours, exercised, and recovered. He completed four operas in rapid succession, but in the midst of renewed acclaim, again suffered major health problems. Once again, he descended to poverty. With no more engagements, Handel appeared defeated and in despair.

This gentle, submissive, tame, patient and humble man would, however, write again. Coming home one evening from a purposeless walk, he found in his room a package—a musical score entitled, "A Sacred Oratorio" written by Charles Jennens. As Handel looked over its pages, God began to do what God can do with one who is meek. Without stopping, Handel charted score after score, often refusing to eat. Exhausted, he finally finished and expressed his elation: "I did think I did see all Heaven before me and the great God himself!" Handel collapsed into a seventeen-hour sleep, while on a nearby table lay the greatest oratorio ever composed, the Messiah. "Blessed are the meek."

REWARD

The resulting promise for the meek is, *"they shall inherit the earth"* (Matthew 5:5). This is almost an exact quote from Psalm 37:11. In the Old Testament, the "earth" refers to the promised land while in the New Testament it refers to all the blessings of God.

I was once involved in the settlement of an inheritance. Some time before death, the relative became ill and in the midst of the illness changed the will. This was not known until after the relative's death when the will was probated. A few other relatives along with myself were left out of the revised will. A contest of the will produced only a minimal out-of-court settlement, much of which went to attorney fees. I was deeply hurt. The monetary loss, although heavy was secondary to the emotional trauma of being left out. The experience, even though painful, helped me appreciate the assurance of my inheritance as a member of the family of God. As a joint-heir with Jesus, I will "inherit a blessing" (1 Peter 3:9).

The earth is not to be possessed, grabbed at, or fought over. It is to be inherited by those who through faith have become joint-heirs with Jesus Christ. "The earth is the Lord's, and all it contains" (Psalm 24:1). George McDonald said, "We cannot see the world as God means it in the future, save as our souls are characterized by meekness. In meekness we are its only inheritors. Meekness alone makes the spiritual retina pure to receive God's things as they are, mingling with them neither imperfection nor impurity."

The earth belongs to the powerless and disenfranchised disciples, and to us. Those who from time to time possess it by force will lose it, for "The kingdom of the world has become the kingdom of our Lord and of His Christ" (Revelation 11:15) and earth is the front porch of "a house not made with hands, eternal in the heavens" (2 Corinthians 5:1). To inherit this earth is to also inherit, "a new heaven and a new earth" (Revelation 21:1).

Therefore, "Seek the Lord, all you meek of the earth" (Zephaniah 2:3, NKJV).

REVIEW

Keeping in mind the meaning of *praus,* what evidences are there of meekness in your life?

1. Lord, show me one evidence of meekness in my life today.

2._____

_____

3._____

_____

4._____

_____

_____

REJOICE

1. Thank You, Lord that the meaning of *praus* is not weak, for I do not wish to be weak, in Your eyes nor in my world-witness.

2._____

_____

_____

3._____

_____

_____

4._____

_____

_____

REPENT

1. Forgive me Lord for taking my biblical meekness for granted and trying to conquer my part of the earth with its use.

2._____

_____

_____

3._____

_____

_____

4._____

_____

_____

REQUEST FOR SELF

1. Lord, what is there to inherit after all, when You own it all and I have all I need? Grant me the wisdom to know what is mine, and the strength to use it only to glorify You.

2._____

_____

_____

3._____

_____

_____

4._____

_____

_____

REQUEST FOR OTHERS

1.   Lord, as You are shaping me into proper meekness, would You grant inheritance qualities to my friend_____.

2._____

_____

_____

3._____

_____

_____

4._____

_____

_____

CHAPTER FOUR: BEING RIGHTEOUS

REFLECT

"Blessed are those who hunger and thirst for righteousness" (Matthew 5:6).

Many of those who heard Jesus speak had made journeys across trackless deserts, hunting one oasis after another, but finding mostly mirages. Without any weather reports or warnings, they would be confronted by gusty wind and stinging sand. The moving sand dunes would cover human tracks and cause them to be disoriented. When they attempted to turn their bodies away from the blinding sand, its thickness would affect their breathing, and become caked in their hair, and on their clothing. Then would come the unquenchable thirst.

History repeated such experiences. Thousands of people threw themselves into the Tiber River to end their lives because of the famine in 436 B.C. in Rome. Similar famine struck England in 1005 and all of Europe in 879, 1016, and 1162. In the nineteenth century hunger attacked Russia, China, India, and Ireland. In recent years parts of India, Africa and Latin America have been devastated by hunger. Millions have died in this decade of hunger and its related diseases.

On a recent three-week prayer journey, our team was to walk for several hours per day in some very hot climates. I tried my best to get in good physical shape before the experience. Even my best efforts were not enough. Nor was it enough to carry plastic water bottles everywhere I went. On a cloudless day, in a middle east country, with the sum beaming down and sweat pouring off my face, I almost dehydrated. It was in this same area, in this same kind of climate, that Jesus talked about thirst to those who understood its meaning.

In an overweight society, where people quench their hunger and thirst by opening the refrigerator door, hunger and thirst have only relative meaning. More than dictionary words, "hunger and thirst" are words that must be experienced—like the words "pain" and "love"—to be fully understood. In a country where the average wage was eight pence per day, the people had experiential knowledge of hunger and thirst. Jesus spoke this attribute to felt needs.

Just as physical hunger and thirst lead to physical necessities of life, so spiritual hunger and thirst lead to spiritual necessities of life. This attribute is not about luxuries. The Psalmist likened these drives to that of the little deer that thirsted for water, "As the deer pants for the water brooks, So my soul pants for You, O God. My soul thirsts for God" (Psalm 42:1-2).

The major difference between physical hunger and thirst and spiritual hunger and thirst is in capacity. In physical hunger and thirst consumption diminishes capacity. I re-learn this difference every time I eat at an all-you-can-eat buffet. When I am full, I can eat or drink no more until I become hungry and thirsty again. In spiritual hunger and thirst consumption increases capacity. The more I take in, the more I desire.

Jesus said he himself would be our spiritual food: "I am the bread of life; he who comes to Me will not hunger, and he who believes in Me will never thirst" (John 6:35). Likewise Jesus said he would supply our spiritual water: "Everyone who drinks of this water [from the well at Sychar] will thirst again; but whoever drinks of the water that I will give him shall never thirst; but the water that I will give him shall become in him a well of water springing up to eternal life" (John 4:13—14). A popular chorus by Martha Stevens says:

Come to the water, stand by my side;

I know you are thirsty, you won't be denied.

Although the word righteousness (*dikaiosune*) sometimes means justice or justification, here the word refers to doing the things God is for and refraining from those things God is against. A family of dinner guests had just sat down at the table to eat when the spoiled little son noticed he didn't want any of the food on the table. Announcing his displeasure, he got up and stormed through a nearby door. Trying to ease the tension, the mother exclaimed, "Well, now that he's gone, we can enjoy this delicious meal in peace." To which the hostess replied, "Oh, he'll be back. He just went into a closet." If we are hungry and thirsty for anything other than what God has for us, we simply close ourselves off from God's best and close ourselves in to a lesser existence. Refusing the things of God is as foolish as the spoiled child storming into a closet.

There are some prerequisites to being truly hungry and thirsty for righteousness. First, we can only be truly hungry and thirsty for righteousness if we are dissatisfied with ourselves spiritually. We know the difference in getting up from a meal fully satisfied with good food versus getting up from a meal where we have eaten something we did not really want and that does not now agree with our digestive system. We are now dissatisfied with ourselves and eager to eat a good meal again. Someone who is self-satisfied spiritually is not a good candidate for desiring right-living with God. In fact, the person who least desires righteousness may be the one who needs it most. We must have a genuine desire to be emancipated from selfish concerns. Like Paul, we must conclude, "Wretched man that I am!" (Romans 7:24). Surely, no person is so empty as the person who thinks he or she is full, but in reality, is full of the wrong thing. Jesus spoke harsh words to a church in this condition, "You say I am rich, and have become wealthy, and have need of nothing: and you do not know that you are wretched and miserable and poor and blind and naked" (Revelation 3:17).

Second, we can only be truly hungry and thirsty for righteousness when we become free from dependence on external things for satisfaction. At the conclusion of a football bowl game, I heard a member of the losing team say to a reporter, "Our fans weren't here and we weren't ever in the game." The athlete is not really hungry for victory until the roar of the crowd becomes secondary to winning. As long as the things of this world bring complete, lasting satisfaction, there can be no desire for righteousness. Paul so desired right living with God he was willing to set aside "a righteousness of my own derived from the Law" in order "that I may know Him" (Philippians 3:9-10). This was not the case with one of Paul's companions, Demas, of whom Paul said, "Having loved this present world, has deserted me" (2 Timothy 4:10).

Third, we can only be truly hungry and thirsty for righteousness if we crave the things of God. After a hard work-out, a long run, or a difficult competition, the physically fit athlete is anxious to eat. No one has to persuade them to eat. Those who are hungry and thirsty do not have to be called to the table repeatedly. Instead, like Isaiah, they cry, "At night my soul longs for You, indeed, my spirit within me seeks You diligently" (Isaiah 26:9) and like the Psalmist they exclaim, "My soul is crushed with longing after Your ordinances at all times" (Psalm 119:20). The person who craves the things of God observes the things of the world and confesses, "Every good thing given and every perfect gift is from above" (James 1:17). Like dead persons who desire no food or water, the person who does not crave for the things of God is most likely "dead in . . . trespasses and sins" (Ephesians 2:1). They go from one earthly side-show to another craving the wrong things.

Fourth, we can only be truly hungry and thirsty for righteousness if we desire to be around the people of God. Have you ever noticed how physical fitness buffs hang out together? They enjoy each other's company. They swap trade secrets and become more physically fit because of the support of like-minded friends. The biblical principal is, "Iron sharpens iron, so one man sharpens another" (Proverbs 27:17). Godless friends provide a good challenge for evangelism and ministry but provide a poor substitute for Christian fellowship. Some of the saddest words written about any disciple are those written on the night of Jesus' resurrection when he appeared to the disciples, "But Thomas, one of the twelve, called Didymus, was not with them when Jesus came" (John 20:24). Among other things, Thomas missed the strength that comes from Christian fellowship. Somewhere Thomas, the doubter, was trying to make it alone.

One word of warning. Avoid impulsive eating or drinking. Instant gratification leads to long term debt. The disciple who desires spiritual fitness must learn to discern between what is spiritually healthy and what is spiritually unhealthy. Just as God made us with a physical appetite that tells us when we are really hungry, so God made us with a spiritual appetite that tells us when we need spiritual nourishment. No one has to explain to a baby that he or she is hungry. It is a created drive. Not so with impulsive eating and drinking. We learn how to yield to this temptation. While on Sabbatical leave in Boston, I discovered a Dunkin' Donut Shop every few blocks and in nearly every subway station. Because I ate donuts impulsively, both my weight and blood pressure went up. It took many months to correct this impulsiveness. We must be careful, spiritually, that we don't jump quickly to some apparent truth that offers instant gratification. It may give us spiritual indigestion.

REWARD

The resulting promise for hungering and thirsting after righteousness is not a reward for achievement but rather a response to an attribute: *"they shall be satisfied"* (Matthew 5:6). The word for satisfied is *chortazesthia* and means to be stuffed, filled to capacity. This word is a passive verb. We do not satisfy ourselves; we are satisfied by God.

The promise is filling to satisfaction. In Greek mythology King Tantalus was punished for offending the gods. As punishment he was placed in a body of water up to his chin. Every time he tried to drink the water receded. Furthermore, choice fruit hung just over his head. Yet when he tried to reach it, it too receded. He became the symbol of teasing and his name provided the root of our word, tantalize. Jesus offers real filling to satisfaction, not teasing. The Bible says, "eat what is good, and delight yourself in abundance" (Isaiah 55:2). Claire Cloniger and Martin J. Nystrom said it this way:

Come to the table of mercy,

Prepared with the wine and the bread

All who are hungry and thirsty,

Come and your souls will be fed.

The encouraging part of this attribute is that spiritual filling is offered not to the one who is already righteous, but to those who are hungry and thirsty for righteousness. The possession is available to those still on the pathway.

Even though we still may hunger and thirst along the way, ultimately, we will feast at the marriage supper of the Lamb (Revelation 19:9) in a place where "They will hunger no more, neither thirst any more" (Revelation 7:16). In that day we shall truly be spiritually fit disciples. Until then we join with that Welsh Methodist, William Williams in singing:

Guide me, O thou great Jehovah,

Pilgrim through this barren land;

I am weak, but thou art mighty;

Hold me with thy powerful hand;

Bread of heaven, Bread of heaven,

Feed me till I want no more,

Feed me till I want no more.

REVIEW

How desperately do you hunger and thirst for righteousness? Can you cite one example of your hunger and thirst?

1. Show me at least one example Lord, of how I hunger and thirst after righteousness.

2._____

_____

_____

3._____

_____

_____

4._____

_____

_____

REJOICE

1. Lord, thank You that while we hunger and thirst after many things, that which we really need, righteousness, is readily available to us.

2._____

_____

_____

3._____

_____

_____

4._____

_____

_____

REPENT

1. Forgive me Lord for hungering and thirsting after food and drink, after security, after success, after popularity, after wealth, after so many things I need less than Your righteousness.

2._____

_____

3._____

_____

4._____

_____

_____

REQUEST FOR SELF

1. Lord, keep me from substituting self-righteousness for Your righteousness.

2._____

_____

_____

3._____

_____

_____

4._____

_____

_____

REQUEST FOR OTHERS

1. Lord, all around me there are those who hunger and thirst for You, and they may not even know it. Today, I am thinking of and interceding on behalf of my friend_____.

2._____

_____

_____

3._____

_____

_____

4._____

_____

_____

CHAPTER FIVE: BEING MERCIFUL

REFLECT

"*Blessed are the merciful*" (Matthew 5:7). In the Old Testament the parallel word is *chesedh*, translated ninety-six times as "mercy" thirty-eight times as "kindness," and thirty times as "lovingkindness." Indeed, "The earth is full of Your loving kindness, O Lord" (Psalm 119:64). Again, God "delights in mercy" (Micah 7:18 NKJV). God showed mercy to Lot in the escape from Sodom (Genesis 19:19) and to Jacob as his life was protected (Genesis 32:10). Furthermore, God extended mercy to Joseph as he rose to power in Egypt (Genesis 39:21) and to David by giving him a son to succeed him as King (2 Samuel 7:12). The Children of Israel experienced God's mercy as they were directed by God (Psalm 106:7).

The word for mercy in the New Testament is *eleos* which is used twenty-seven times. Whereas in the Old Testament the idea was outgoing kindness, in the New Testament the idea contained in this word is outgoing love, the opposite of self-centeredness. It is not just an emotion, but emotion with action. "God so loved" is an emotion, but "God so loved the world, that He gave His only begotten Son" (John 3:16) is actualized outgoing love. Michael W. Smith wrote:

Great is the Lord, He is faithful and true;

By His mercy He proves He is love.

Jesus further illustrated this attribute in the parable of the Good Samaritan, when He said of the Samaritan, who had discovered a beaten man by the road:

A Samaritan, who was on a journey, came upon him; and when he saw him, he felt compassion, and came to him, and bandaged up his wounds, pouring oil and wine on them; and he put him on his own beast, and brought him to an inn and took care of him. (Luke 10:33-34)

Mercy is shown to the one who is wrong, as in the story of the unmerciful slave (Matthew 18:23-35) and also shown to the one who is in need, as in blind Bartimaeus crying, "Jesus, Son of David, have mercy on me!" (Mark 10:47). Further, the New Testament teaches us that God is "rich in mercy, because of His great love with which He loved us" (Ephesians 2:4); that God invites us to, "draw near with confidence to the throne of grace, that we may receive mercy" (Hebrews 4:16); that we have a living hope, "according to His great mercy" (1 Peter 1:3); and finally that we are to "Be merciful, just as your Father is merciful" (Luke 6:3 6).

Mercy does not characterize our world. Today the world prefers to insulate itself against the pain and hurt of humanity Today the world exacts revenge and shuns forgiveness.

Napoleon was moved by a mother's plea for a pardon on behalf of her son. Napoleon responded that it was the young man's second offense. The second offense and justice demanded death. The mother responded, "I do not ask for justice, I plead for mercy." To which Napoleon replied, "But he does not deserve mercy." "Sire," she cried, "it would not be mercy if he deserved it, and mercy is all I ask for." Napoleon granted the pardon on the basis of mercy.

A student of mine shared a story from his days as a High School quarterback. It was the biggest football game of his senior season. His team was behind by four points with time enough for only one play before the first half ended. The coach called for a pass play My student, the quarterback, rolled out and threw a perfect pass to the wide receiver. The opposing player who was defending this wide receiver, fell down. The wide receiver was wide open and all alone. No one was between him and the goal line. A half-time lead was in everyone's minds. But the wide receiver dropped the ball. All through the half-time break, no one in the locker room spoke to the wide receiver. He was sure that his playing days were over. As the team prepared to leave the locker room for the second half, the coach surprised everyone by announcing that this same wide receiver who cost his team a half-time lead would be starting at wide receiver in the second half. He deserved justice. He received mercy. He also scored the winning touchdown late in the game to give his school the victory.

When the reality of our mistakes begin to overwhelm us, the truth of God's mercy rescues us. The old hymn by William R. Newell says it this way:

By God's Word at last my sin I learned;

Then I trembled at the law I'd spurned,

Till my guilty soul imploring turned To Calvary.

Mercy there was great, and grace was free;

Pardon there was multiplied to me;

There my burdened soul found liberty at Calvary.

How then can we who are recipients of such outgoing love show mercy to others? First, we show mercy through concern for others. Because we have experienced God's great mercy, we should be concerned for those who never or seldom experience it. Even on the cross, Jesus showed merciful concern to the repentant thief (Luke 23:43) who with dry throat and collapsing muscles was painfully paying for his crime against society. Then he showed mercy to his mother (John 19:26-27) whose grief was mixed with thoughts of an uncertain future with no husband and now no oldest son. Finally, he showed mercy to those who were killing him (Luke 23:34) who even in their military discipline may have questioned the implementing of these orders.

Second, we show mercy by striving to right social wrongs. Jesus fed the hungry, restored the disenfranchised, condemned the corrupt leaders, befriended the friendless, healed the sick, and challenged the prejudiced. Can we do any less? Mercy allows us to see from another's perspective, think with another's mind, and feel with another's emotions. It is much deeper than sympathy. It is empathy followed by action on another's behalf. It "seasons justice" as William Shakespeare wrote in The Merchant of Venice:

The quality of mercy is not strain'd,

It droppeth as the gentle rain from heaven

Upon the place beneath: it is twice bless'd;

It blesseth him that gives and him that takes:

"Tis mightiest in the mightiest; it becomes

The throned monarch better than his crown;

His sceptre shows the force of temporal power,

The attribute to awe and majesty,

Wherein doth sit the dread and fear of kings;

But mercy is above the sceptred sway,

It is enthroned in the hearts of kings,

It is an attribute to God himself,

And earthly power doth then show likest God's

When mercy seasons justice.

Third, we show mercy by sharing the gospel with the unsaved. When humankind fell, God immediately activated a prearranged plan of redemption, culminating in the greatest act of outgoing love, the death of Christ on the cross. Paul says, "He saved us, not on the basis of deeds which we have done in righteousness, but according to His mercy" (Titus 3:5). That saving mercy is available to all. When our lives are touched by the magnificent mercy of God, we should willingly share it with others.

REWARD

The resulting promise here is that the one who is merciful "*shall receive mercy*" (Matthew 5:7). Later in this same sermon Jesus said, "In the way you judge, you will be judged" (Matthew 7:2) and James added, "Judgement will be merciless to one who has shown no mercy" (James 2:13).

This then is God's way: If you would have truth, you must be true; if you would have love, you must love; if you would have friendship, you must be a friend; if you would have mercy, you must be merciful. Your willingness to show mercy is part of the prerequisite in receiving it.

Charles Haddon Spurgeon said, "God will measure us with our own check-lists." No beatitude makes this clearer. We are the result, we make the result, and we become the result.

An inscription on a tombstone in an Aberdeen churchyard speaks of mercy received and mercy given.

Here lie I, Martin Elginbrodde;

Ha'e mercy o' my soul, Lord God;

As I wad do, were I Lord God,

An' ye were Martin Elginbrodde.

In his plays Adronacles and the Lion, George Bernard Shaw portrays his character walking through a jungle and meeting a lion in great pain with an infected thorn in its paw Due to his condition, the lion was too weak to be dangerous. The man took out the thorn, poured alcohol in the wound, and went on his way. Years later the man, a Christian, was thrown into an arena of lions. One lion recognized him, nestled up against him, and protected him from the others. Mercy was shown to the merciful.

Ultimately, in addition to the mercy we are shown on this earth, Jude encourages us to "keep yourselves in the love of God, waiting anxiously for the mercy of our Lord Jesus Christ to eternal life" (Jude 21).

REVIEW

Keeping in mind the meanings of the words translated as merciful, what is one way you can express mercy to someone else today? How have you received mercy this week from God? From another person? Give thanks right now for mercy received.

1. Lord, please bring to my attention whoever in my day needs mercy,

   then help me to show it.

2._____

_____

_____

3._____

_____

_____

4._____

_____

_____

REJOICE

1. Thank You, Lord, that even though I am not a Judge, or a President, or a General, or a person with such authority, I can nevertheless show mercy.

2._____

_____

_____

3._____

_____

_____

4._____

_____

_____

REPENT

1. Forgive me Lord for having the ability to show mercy, while often failing to do so.

2._____

_____

_____

3._____

_____

_____

4._____

_____

_____

REQUEST FOR SELF

1. Lord, You have shown mercy to me when I least deserved it, please continue to do so, for I fear I may need it again soon, and not deserve it.

2._____

_____

_____

3._____

_____

_____

4._____

_____

_____

REQUEST FOR OTHERS

1. Lord, You know that special friend of mine whose actions do not deserve mercy. Help me to be more like You than like myself, and thus show mercy to_____

2._____

_____

_____

3._____

_____

_____

4._____

_____

_____

CHAPTER SIX: BEING PURE IN HEART

REFLECT

"*Blessed are the pure in heart*" (Matthew 5:8). The word pure, *katharos,* means clean, unmixed, unadulterated, unalloyed. The word appears twenty-eight times in the New Testament and refers to rightness of mind and singleness of motive. This attribute begins by saying, blessed are those whose thoughts and motives are absolutely unmixed, free from foreign matter, and therefore pure.

The significance of purity vs. impurity is illustrated by Alfred Lord Tennyson's two knights of the Round Table. Impurity barred the vision of Sir Lancelot and kept him from seeing the Holy Grail, the cup thought to be the symbol and vehicle of the blood of Jesus. Tennyson says of Lancelot, all that was "pure, noble, and knightly" in him "twined and clung 'round that one sin, until the wholesome flower and poisonous grew together, each as each, not to be plucked asunder." Because what is in our heart determines what we see, Lancelot was not even able to see the Holy Grail when he came to Castle Carbonek, but as he looked in its direction, "a stormy glare, a heat as from a seven- times heated furnace, blasted and burnt and blinded him."

On the other hand, Tennyson has Galahad, the pure knight say, "My strength is as of ten, because my heart is pure." While Lancelot was brave in battle, Galahad was pure in heart.

The Bible speaks of six different kinds of purity. There is that divine purity that exists only in and is essential to God's character. Similar to divine purity is created purity such as God established in creation prior to the fall of humankind. Imputed purity is given to us at the time of our conversion. This kind of purity is often called righteousness in the New Testament (Romans 4:5; 2 Corinthians 5:21) and in the songs we sing like the one by Don Harris:

Lord, make me pure in heart.

Make my heart faithful and true.

So, when you look at me

It's your righteousness You see.

Lord, make me pure in heart.

Along with imputed purity God gives renewed purity. In other words, as we sin against God, God allows us to be renewed again and again (Romans 6:4-5; 8:5-11; Colossians 3:9-10; 1. Peter 1:3). There is also a shared purity mentioned in the New Testament, in which we participate with God in our own purity Paul calls us to "cleanse ourselves from all defilement of flesh and spirit, perfecting holiness in the fear of God" (2 Corinthians 7:1) and Peter adds, "Do not be conformed to the former lusts which were yours in ignorance, but like the Holy One who called you, be holy yourselves also in all your behavior" (1 Peter 1:14-16).

Finally, there will be rewarded purity which we will experience in heaven for "we will be like Him, because we will see Him just as He is" (1 John 3:2).

The idea of pure in heart puts all else in proper priority. You can't live a pure life without a pure heart. Many try to work this formula backwards, but pure life does not result in a pure heart. Rather a pure heart results in a pure life; that is, a life that is unmixed with evil. Just as pure gold is without alloy and pure water is free from other liquids or matter, so a pure heart is one with no mixture. Thus, it is single-minded and focused. As Kierkegaard reminded us, "Purity of heart is to will one will."

We live in a day of enormous knowledge and concern about the human heart. This rugged, four-valved, four-chambered pump organ handles 5,000 gallons of blood per day, enough to fill a railroad tank car. This amazing organ supplies the human circulatory system through 12,000 miles of vessels. In the course of an average lifetime it beats 2,500,000 times.

We speak often of the heart in phrases like "his heart is in the right place," referring to motives; "have a heart," referring to emotions; "open up your heart," when appealing to someone to not be harsh or hard; "hard-hearted," when referring to personality; "she's got heart," when referring to energy or activity or describing one as being non-passive; "think about this in your heart," when referring to the mental. Thus, "heart" becomes a synonym for the whole person.

In the New Testament times, medical science was still of the belief that blood carried thought, concluding then that all thought originated in the heart. Thus, to the Hebrew, the heart included intellect, emotions, and will. This led to the biblical idea, "For as he thinks in his heart, so is he" (Proverbs 23:7, NKJV). As well as the question of Jesus, "Why are you thinking evil in your hearts?" (Matthew 9:4). Likewise the question, "Why are you reasoning about these things in your hearts?" (Mark 2:8). Of the 148 uses of the New Testament word heart, *kardia,* almost all refer to the inner person.

Even in our day, with so much emphasis on heart care, heart by-pass, and heart transplants, there is so little concern for heart purity The Bible is clear in its statements concerning the importance of heart purity: "Watch over your heart with all diligence" (Proverbs 4:23) implores the writer of the Proverbs. The Psalmist prays, "Create in me a clean heart, O God" (Psalm 51:10), and Jesus adds, "For from within, out of the heart of men, proceed the evil thoughts" (Mark 7:21).

Again, purity of heart is an inward thing. In the world of Jesus' day purity was a matter of ritual observance, obedience to a list of rules and regulations, a ceremonial matter. On the Day of Atonement, the high priest washed his entire body five times and his hands ten times. Before a meal, orthodox Jews first poured water over their hands with fingers pointed upward, then with fingers pointed downward, then washed each palm by rubbing it with the fist of the other hand.

Jesus set the proper order by beginning purity on the inside. Nothing on the outside can change us on the inside -- not government, not family, not education, not morality, not religion, not behavior modification, not twelve steps, not rehabilitation, and not therapy -- only that which is in our heart. No wonder the writer of the Proverbs implored us to "watch over your heart with all diligence, for," he adds "from it flow the springs of life" (Proverbs 4:23). Unfortunately, this wellspring of life has become a polluted spring that only God can make pure.

Purity of heart comes by allowing God to control your thoughts. Early in human history, "the Lord saw that the wickedness of man was great on the earth, and that every intent of the thoughts of his heart was only evil continually" (Genesis 6:5). Temptations are brilliant but often deadly, scenery is bewitching but often corrupting. We must allow no thought to remain in our mind that taints or defiles God's purity. We must heed Paul's encouragement, "whatever is true, whatever is honorable, whatever is right, whatever is pure, whatever is lovely, whatever is of good repute. . . dwell on these things" (Philippians 4:8). I have found it helpful to turn to prayer when an impure thought tries to invade my mind. This places God back in control of my thoughts. Robert Browning said it well: "Thought is the soul of the act."

Likewise, purity of heart comes by allowing God to control your affections. We must love. We have been created to love. But we must not allow our affectionate love to stray to those to whom we ought not give it whether this be expressed in monopolizing friendships, exclusive relationships, or adulterous involvement. Common sense, if followed, will lead us away from impure affections.

Purity of heart comes also by allowing God to control your will. Impurity often springs from the lack of a resolute will or a wavering on decisions. Like the front wheels of a front-wheel drive vehicle, a will controlled by God must steer our course and set our direction.

As God controls our thoughts, our affections, our wills, and makes our hearts pure our actions will become pure. Just changing the filters in your air conditioning system will not help much if the source of the air is polluted. Neither will a variety of activities produce pure action unless the heart is purified by God.

We are not talking about sinless perfection. The Bible tells of Noah getting drunk, Abraham deceiving King Abimelech, Moses disobeying God, Job cursing the day of his birth, Elijah fleeing in fear, Peter denying Christ, and Paul confessing his tendency to evil when he wanted to do good. None were perfect or sinless, but all were pure in heart. Just because an athlete makes a costly mistake does not make him or her any less a member of the team. Likewise, even though a spiritual athlete sins, they are still a part of the faith team.

REWARD

The resulting reward is *"they shall see God"* (Matthew 5:8). While impurity obscures our vision of God, purity enhances that vision. To see God must surely be one of the ultimate purposes of a disciple. Yet it is only the disciple, the pure in heart, who can see God. The impure of heart see everything but God. What one is determines what one sees, and that which we miss seeing stems from the things we miss being. The more God-like we become, the more of God we see in other people, in creation, and obviously in the scripture.

So, the pure in heart do see God, because of who we are. This has always been true -- what one sees is determined by what one is. In Jesus' day the rich man could purchase an unblemished lamb for sacrifice while the poor man purchased a dove. But whether rich or poor, the pure in heart were the ones who worshiped God. Physical eyes saw lambs and doves. Spiritual eyes saw the Lord. Yard workers see trees as leaf producers. Golfers see trees as obstacles. However, Joyce Kilmer wrote:

I think that I shall never see

A poem as lovely as a tree.

Perhaps the point is best illustrated by the poem of the pussycat who went to London. Upon return, the cat was asked:

Pussy cat, pussy cat, where have you been?

I've been to London to visit the Queen.

Pussy cat, pussy cat what saw you there?

I saw a little mouse under a chair.

Cats are cats. They see mice, even in the presence of royalty. The spiritually unfit disciple who is impure of heart sees the impure, even in the midst of purity. They even come to church and complain of not experiencing God there. Only the pure in heart see God. They see wonder in each week, deity in each day, holiness in each hour, majesty in every moment, and the sacred in each second.

It was the desire of Old Testament saints to see God. Moses cried, "I pray You, show me Your glory!" (Exodus 33:18). David exclaimed, "As the deer pants for the water brooks, So my soul pants for You, O God" (Psalm 42:1). Job confessed, "I have heard of You by the hearing of the ear; But now my eye sees You" (Job 42:5). We join their desire in wanting to see God. It is absolutely amazing to me the ends to which people will go to see God. They will crawl on bloody knees, starve themselves, endure seasons of separation from friends, and grasp at any fresh idea, just to see God. Even in our music we acknowledge our desire to see God. Keith Green wrote:

O Lord, You're beautiful.

Your face is all I seek.

For when Your eyes are on this child,

Your grace abounds to me.

The promise of seeing God is both present and future. John assures us, "Beloved, now we are children of God, and it has not appeared as yet what we will be. We know that when He appears, we will be like Him, because we will see Him just as He is" (1 John 3:2). Again, John tells us "He is coming with the clouds, and every eye will see Him" (Revelation 1:7). Once again, of those in heaven John says, "They will see His face" (Revelation 22:4). F. E Bullard has expressed the ultimate goal by writing:

When I in righteousness at last

Thy glorious face shall see;

When all the weary night has passed,

And I awake with Thee,

To view the glories that abide,

Then and only then will I be satisfied.

What will it be like for us to see Jesus? We will see a brow where a crown of thorns once pierced the skin. We will see a face from which some of the beard was plucked out. We will see hands and feet that were once pierced with nails. We will see a side once opened with a sword. We will see eyes that never saw a person beyond hope. We will see lips through which came words so meaningful, that volumes have been written to explain them. We will see ears worthy of hearing our praise. We will see our joint-heir to the Kingdom. We will see our advocate with the Father. We will see the One whom to see is to see the Father. We will see the One who did not leave us comfortless. We will see the object of all our hallelujahs. We will see what we have been striving to become.

Alfred Lord Tennyson was once asked, "What is your greatest wish?" He responded, "A clear vision of God." Perhaps this is why, on his deathbed, he instructed his oldest son to see that "Crossing the Bar" would be the final poem in any future collection of his works. The poem ends:

For tho' from out our bourne of Time and Place

The tide may bear me far,

I hope to see my Pilot face to face

When I have crossed the bar.

REVIEW

Review the different kinds of purity in the Bible. What are your needs related to renewed purity? Related to shared purity? Ask God what is necessary for each to be enhanced in your life. How have you seen: wonder in this week? deity in this day? holiness in this hour? majesty in this moment?

1. Lord, I can only see You through the purity that You offer me, purity that counteracts my own impurity.

2._____

_____

_____

3._____

_____

_____

4._____

_____

_____

REJOICE

1. Thank You, Lord for the purity that You offer that overcomes the impurities in my life.

2._____

_____

_____

3._____

_____

_____

4._____

_____

_____

REPENT

1. Forgive me Lord for entertaining and even enjoying the impurities of life, when You offer purity to me.

2._____

_____

_____

3._____

_____

_____

4._____

_____

_____

REQUEST FOR SELF

1. Lord, I desire to see You in all Your glory, so please keep me pure that I may have my desire.

2._____

_____

_____

3._____

_____

_____

4._____

_____

_____

REQUEST FOR OTHERS

1. Lord, seeing You, enables me to better show You to others, so grant me the purity needed to show You to my friend

   _____

2. _____

   _____

   _____

3. _____

   _____

   _____

4. _____

   _____

   _____

CHAPTER SEVEN: BEING A PEACEMAKER

REFLECT

" *Blessed are the peacemakers*" (Matthew 5:9). Used eighty-eight times in the New Testament, the word peace appears in all twenty-seven books. Indeed, the Bible opens with peace in the Garden of Eden and closes with peace in the eternal city. The gospel opens with peace as the multitude of the heavenly host praise God, saying, "Glory to God in the highest, and on earth peace among men" (Luke 2:14). Before his death, Jesus' last will and testament left "peace" to the disciples (John 14:27) and in one of his first resurrection appearances Jesus greeted his disciples with the words, "Peace be with you" (John 20:19). The Bible is a book of peace, best modeled by Jesus himself.

In all the New Testament, the word peacemaker, *eirenopolis*, appears only here. In the first six beatitudes, blessedness was dependent on an inward condition. Here blessedness is linked to a pro-active involvement. A peacemaker is one who seeks to make peace, not one who simply and passively endures in a posture of peace. This calls for toiling laboriously, living dangerously, fighting sacrificially, and enduring painfully. The tasks of peace are more difficult than those of war, for it is easier to defeat an enemy than to defeat his enmity, easier to stop a fight than to solve the disagreement.

We must remember also that the world in which Jesus first spoke these words was not in peace. It was marked by mutual hatred between Jews and Romans. The Province of Galilee was a revolution waiting to happen. Now the disciples are told they must not only have peace, which they received when they received Jesus as Messiah, but they must also make peace in a troubled world. The disciple always pays a price to make peace.

The disciples would begin, where we must begin, by making peace with self. While it appears this attribute has more to do with conduct than character, it assumes a peacemaker to be a possessor of the attitude of peace. This explains why purity of heart precedes peacemaking. Thomas a Kempis said it well: "First keep thyself in peace, and then thou shalt be able to keep peace among others."

So, not only must disciples make peace with self, but likewise make peace with others. In a day when many are concerned with piece-making (diversity), disciples must be caught up in peacemaking (unity). We are called to be arbitrators for the Almighty, mediators for the Master in the home, workplace, community, church, and place of leisure. We must combat prejudice, competition, jealousy, and envy. There is a New Year's Eve custom in Scotland called "first-footing it." This refers to the first person to enter one's house after midnight to wish a happy new year. It relates to aggressive discipleship -- "first-footing it" for peace.

But the disciple must also make peace with God. Henry David Thoreau was asked near the end of his life if he had made peace with God. He replied, "We never quarreled." I don't know how many of us can say that, but we all should be at peace with God. The Bible instructs us, "do not stiffen your neck like your fathers, but yield to the Lord and enter His sanctuary which He has consecrated forever, and serve the Lord your God, that His burning anger may turn away from you" (2 Chronicles 30:8). We must surrender to God. We must stop fighting God and begin serving God if we would be at peace with God. We are not sons of God because we make peace, rather we make peace because we are sons of God.

When we are at peace with self, others, and God, there will be a greater chance for peace in the world. A Chinese proverb says, "If there is righteousness in the heart, there will be beauty in the character. If there is beauty in the character, there will be harmony in the home. If there is harmony in the home, there will be order in the nation. And when there is order in the nation, there will be peace in the world."

So then, how do we go about making peace? First, we must control our verbal response to situations. Sometimes what we desire to say needs to remain unsaid. Other times what we desire to say needs to be softened and tempered. Our words can disrupt or soothe depending on when and how we use them. An ancient proverb says, "If you talk with a soft voice, you do not need a thick stick." Solomon said it this way, "A gentle answer turns away wrath, but a harsh word stirs up anger" (Proverbs 15:1). James instructs, "Everyone be quick to hear, slow to speak and slow to anger" (James 1:19).

Second, we must control our response to unpeaceful situations. To be used as a peacemaker is often costly. The world's ultimate peace, the peace that passes all human understanding, came from a costly cross: "For it was the Father's good pleasure for all the fullness to dwell in Him, and through Him to reconcile all things to Himself, having made peace through the blood of His cross" (Colossians 1:19-20). The hands that reach to calm the storm were nail-pierced. The feet that go before and pave the way to peace are likewise, nail-pierced.

Martin Luther often told the story of two goats who met on a narrow bridge over deep water. "They could not go back; they durst not fight. After a short parley, one of them lay down and let the other go over him, and thus no harm was done. The moral is easy: Be content if thy person be trod upon for peace's sake. Thy person, I say, not thy conscience." Peacemakers are more concerned with principles than their own person.

Response often finds us reaching out to persons who are resistant to us. Being blessed as peacemakers, we are prone to take the opposite view of others and say, "cursed are the peace- breakers." But this is not the way of the cross. Edwin Markham, author of the poems "The Man with the Hoe" and "Lincoln," was once asked what he considered his greatest poem. Without hesitation he responded, "I wrote four lines which I treasure more than all else I wrote during my entire life:"

He drew a circle that shut me out--

Heretic, rebel, a thing of flout.

But love and I had a wit to win:

We drew a circle that took him in.

Markham's lines show the spirit of a peacemaker.

REWARD

The resulting promise is *"They shall be called sons of God"* (Matthew 5:9). One emphasis is on the word *"called."* We become sons of God at the time of our conversion, but we shall be called sons of God as we pass on the peace we find in Christ. To be made a son of God is to be renewed in God's image and likeness. To be called a son of God is to be recognized and honored as such.

Note we are "sons," *huiroi*, not children of God. In Jewish thought sons bore the meaning of "partaker of the character of." To be called "Sons of Thunder" as James and John were (Mark 3:17) meant they possessed characteristics of thunder. Thus, a son of God possesses God's character.

God is a God of peace. Paul calls God, "the God of peace" (Romans 16:20, 2 Corinthians 13:11, Philippians 4:9) repeatedly as does the writer of Hebrews (Hebrews 13:20). Perhaps there is nothing so God-like as to be a maker of peace. When we lose sight of the Fatherhood of God, it effects the brotherhood of man. When we make peace with our brothers and sisters, we exalt the Fatherhood of God, as sons.

Interestingly enough, the adjective used in this beatitude for peacemaker is the same word used in verb form for the Son of God "establishing peace" in Ephesians 2:15 and "having made peace" in Colossians 1:20. In other words as sons of God and peacemakers, we celebrate our identity also as joint-heir with the Son of God who likewise makes peace and who "Himself is our peace" (Ephesians 2:14).

"Sons of God" is more than just a present label or name since it has future implications as well. "Shall be called" is a continuous future passive tense indicating that throughout eternity, we will be called "sons of God." While we may have a lack of peace here on earth, there awaits for earth's peacemakers an eternity of peace. So, we pray with Francis of Assisi:

Lord, make me an instrument of Your peace:

Where there is hatred, let me sow love;

where there is injury, pardon;

where there is doubt, faith;

where there is despair, hope;

where there is darkness, light; and

where there is sadness, joy.

O divine Master, grant that I may not so much seek

to be consoled as to console;

to be understood as to understand,

to be loved as to love;

For it is in giving that we receive;

it is in pardoning that we are pardoned; and

it is in dying that we are born to eternal life!

REVIEW

A peacemaker is one who seeks to make peace, not one who simply and passively endures in a posture of peace. What have you done or hope to do to be pro-active for peace?

1. Lord I want to be a peacemaker, although I am often more of a piece-maker.

2._____

_____

3._____

_____

4._____

_____

REJOICE

1. Thank You, Lord for allowing me the possibility of being at peace with myself, with others, but most of all, with You.

2._____

_____

3._____

_____

4._____

_____

REPENT

1. Forgive me Lord for often acting more like a baby son, than a grown-up son of Yours.

2._____

_____

_____

3._____

_____

_____

4._____

_____

_____

REQUEST FOR SELF

1. Lord, if I could just make and keep peace with myself, I could do a better job of making peace with others. Help me, please.

2._____

_____

_____

3._____

_____

_____

4._____

_____

_____

REQUEST FOR OTHERS

1. Lord, it is so good being a "son of God". I desire it for others, so help me share this relationship effectively with

   my friend_____.

2._____

   _____

   _____

3._____

   _____

   _____

4._____

   _____

   _____

CHAPTER EIGHT: BEING PERSECUTED

REFLECT

"*Blessed are those who have been persecuted*" (Matthew 5:10). The word persecuted, *dioko*, means "put to flight, driven away and pursued." It is a natural follow-up to making peace. The blessed one is the one who endures hardship rather than the one who weakly abandons convictions. Some believe this beatitude was addressed only to the twelve disciples since they alone would understand its full meaning. Nevertheless, one who lives consistently according to the first seven beatitudes eventually experiences this eighth beatitude.

Jesus told his disciples at a later time, "If you were of the world, the world would love its own: but because you are not of the world, but I chose you out of the world, therefore the world hates you. . . . If they persecuted Me, they will also persecute you" (John 15:19-20). Paul added, "For to you it has been granted for Christ's sake, not only to believe in Him, but also to suffer for His sake" (Philippians 1:29). And again, Paul wrote, "All who desire to live godly in Christ Jesus will be persecuted "(2 Timothy 3:12).

What had been written and spoken came to pass. The early Christians were hated because they were different. Their religion was declared illegal. Because they refused to acknowledge Caesar as Lord, their faith was considered subversive. They lost their jobs, homes, families, and were imprisoned and martyred for their belief. Their goodness was a constant, unspoken condemnation of others' way of life. Just as those who are physically fit offer a silent condemnation to those who are physically unfit, so it is in spiritual fitness.

The only one of the eight beatitudes to be expounded on by Jesus was done to prepare his disciples for future persecution and even death by the time of Acts 7. Jesus promised it, the disciples experienced it, the New

Testament documents it, and the early church felt it. Nor did the persecution end with the disciples.

In his account of Nero's persecution, Tacitus tells of some of the horrors faced by early believers: "Besides being put to death, they were made to serve as objects of amusement; they were clad in the hides of beasts and torn to death by dogs; others were crucified, others set on fire to serve to eliminate the darkness of the night."

In The Martyrdom of Polycarp, a voice from heaven spoke to the aged saint as he was being brought to the stadium to die: "Be strong Polycarp, and play the man." When the Proconsul urged the old man to curse Christ and live, Polycarp replied, "Eighty and six years have I served him, and he hath done me no wrong, how then can I blaspheme my king, who saved me?" Before nailing him to the stake the Proconsul threatened Polycarp with wild beasts and with fire. Rejecting all threats, Polycarp proclaimed, "Let me be as I am. He that granted me to endure the fire will grant me also to remain at the pyre unmoved, without being secured with nails."

Adoniram Judson suffered greatly in stocks while imprisoned in Burma. After his release he asked the King for permission to preach in a particular city. The King responded, "I am willing for a dozen preachers to go to that city, but not you. Not with those hands. My people are not fools enough to listen to and follow your words, but they will not be able to resist those scarred hands." Persecuted, he bore in his body the marks of Jesus.

Few have understood persecution better than Dietrich Bonhoeffer. After much suffering, he was executed by direct order of Heinrich Himmler in April of 1945 in the Flossenburg concentration camp only a few days before it was liberated. Bonhoeffer had written, "Suffering, then, is the badge of true discipleship. The disciple is not above his master. Following Christ means . . . suffering because we have to suffer."

Martin Luther considered suffering among the marks of the true church, and one of the memoranda drawn up in preparation for the Augsburg confession defines the church as the community of those "who are persecuted and martyred for the gospel's sake" and martyred they were.

So many believers were martyred for their faith that by the end of the first Christian century the word for witness and the word for martyr had become the same Greek word, *martus*. A witness in that day had every chance to become a martyr. In fact, the "Gloria Patri" is based on the march-to-death song of the early Christian martyrs.

Then Jesus broadened the scope of persecution with the words, *"Blessed are you when people insult you, and persecute you, and falsely say all kinds of evil against you"* (Matthew 5:11). This personalizes persecution -- no longer the third person "those" of verse 10, but the second person "you" of verse 11.

More than physical torture, this persecution now includes character assassination, insult, spoken malice, ridicule, belittling, and a host of other indignities suffered in families, workplaces, recreation locations, classrooms, and even churches. Modern disciples are reviled like Moses (Exodus 5:21, 14:11, 16:2, 17:2), Samuel (1 Samuel 8:5), Elijah (1 Kings 18:17, 19:2), Micaiah (2 Chronicles 18:17), and Nehemiah (Nehemiah 4). Like the stoning of Stephen, the imprisonment of Peter and John, and the beheading of John the Baptist, today's disciples are persecuted. On a recent three-week prayer journey through the unreached people groups of the world, I visited with pastors, lay-leaders, and new Christians who had been persecuted for their faith. They told stories of friends and fellow-workers who had disappeared and are assumed to be in prison or dead. Many others are presently suffering from lesser forms of persecution.

Yet persecution is a compliment, twice-blessed by our Lord. Persecution means someone takes you seriously. No one persecutes an ineffective, indecisive person. It comes only to those who are considered by others as dangerous and gives the disciple an opportunity to demonstrate he or she is not ashamed of the gospel. Even though we may never become a martyr or even endure heavy persecution, we must agree with W. C. Burns who wrote, Oh, to have a martyr's heart if not a martyr's crown," and with Isaac Watts who asked:

Must I be carried to the skies

On flowery beds of ease,

While others fought to win the prize,

And sailed through bloody seas?

It is not just persecution or being reviled and spoken against, for many endure this, but *"for the sake of righteousness"* (Matthew 5:10) and *"because of Me"* (Matthew 5:11) says Jesus. Persecution in and of itself brings no blessing. It is the object that blesses. We are blessed because of "righteousness" and "because of" our loyalty to Jesus. We suffer not in vain, for "even if you should suffer for the sake of righteousness, you are blessed" (1 Peter 3:14).

It is for righteousness sake that we endure persecution not for lack of wisdom or discernment, not for foolish actions, not for playing with temptation, not for being a fanatic, not even for being faithful to church activities, not for a cause, not for a pet project, not for being good or noble or self-sacrificing, but for righteousness we suffer.

Our commitment is to a person, not a principle; to a man, not a method; to a Savior, not a system; to a Lord, not a list; to a Christ, not a creed. And so, "because of" Jesus, we endure persecution. This, in turn, builds spiritual muscle just as aerobic exercises of resistance build physical muscle. Spiritual muscle will then help us not only resist Satan's attacks, but also stand firm in the midst of further persecution.

"For so they persecuted the prophets who were before you" (Matthew 5:12). There is a plaque at Boulder Dam upon which are listed the names of those who died during its construction. It reads, "These have made the desert to blossom like a rose." Many are blessed because some suffer. The joy of the difficult way lies in its fellowship. The pathway of persecution is hallowed by the footsteps of God's saints and God's Son, who "endured the cross, despising the shame" (Hebrews 12:2).

"Rejoice, and be glad" (Matthew 5:12). Jesus endured his persecution, "for the joy set before Him" (Hebrews 12:2). Peter tells us, "to the

degree that you share the sufferings of Christ, keep on rejoicing" (1 Peter 4:13). How do we respond to our persecution? We do not sulk like a child, nor lick our wounds like a dog, nor grin and bear it like a Stoic, nor pretend to enjoy it like a masochist. We rejoice.

We rejoice like Paul because "we are afflicted in every way, but not crushed; perplexed, but not despairing; persecuted, but not forsaken; struck down, but not destroyed; always carrying about in the body the dying of Jesus, that the life of Jesus also may be manifested in our body" (2 Corinthians 4:8-10).

REWARD

The resulting rewards were, *"For theirs is the kingdom of heaven"* (Matthew 5:10); and *"for your reward in heaven is great"* (Matthew 5:12). Here is the final reward but with present connotations. We do not enter the kingdom of God because of our successful endurance of persecution. We are persecuted and will ultimately enjoy the reward because we are presently a part of the kingdom of heaven. There is no reward in self-sought persecution or martyrdom. He who is thrown to the lions is a persecuted martyr on his way to great heavenly reward. He who jumps into the den is a self-seeking egotist who already has his reward.

Make no mistake, there is a reward! Paul promised, "We suffer with Him so that we may also be glorified with Him" (Romans 8:17) and "If we endure, we shall also reign with Him" (2 Timothy 2:12). Moses chose "rather to endure ill-treatment with the people of God than to enjoy the passing pleasures of sin, considering the reproach of Christ greater riches than the treasures of Egypt; for he was looking to the reward" (Hebrews 11:25-26).

A most unusual evergreen tree grows in Yellowstone National Park, the lodgepole pine. Like other pines, its cones remain on the tree for years. Even when they do fall off, they usually remain unopen. They open only when exposed to extreme heat such as a forest fire. Frequently, following a devastating fire, the first tree to grow again in the fire-ravaged area is the lodgepole pine. What devastates some, brings life to others. Out of heavy persecution, comes the disciple's reward of eternal life.

REVIEW

Keeping in mind the meaning of the word *dioko*, persecuted, how have you experienced this in the past few days? What is one way you can rejoice right now in the midst of your persecutions?

1. Lord, I am humbled and honored to be part of the same forever family with biblical characters who were persecuted for the sake of the gospel.

2._____

_____

_____

3._____

_____

_____

4._____

_____

_____

REJOICE

1. Lord. even though my "persecution" is mild compared to others, I thank You for the long list of those who have preceded me.

2._____

_____

_____

3._____

_____

_____

4._____

_____

_____

REPENT

1. Forgive me Lord for complaining when my "persecution" pales in comparison to those saints who have gone before me.

2._____

_____

_____

3._____

_____

_____

4._____

_____

_____

REQUEST FOR SELF

1. Lord, as I enjoy "the power of . . . resurrection" give me strength to endure "the fellowship of . . . suffering (Philippians 3:10).

2._____

_____

_____

3. _____

_____

_____

4. _____

_____

_____

REQUEST FOR OTHERS

1. The paradox that allows witness to come through pain, is amazing to

me, Lord. Whatever pain I suffer, may it be used as a witness,

especially to_____

2._____

_____

_____

3._____

_____

4._____

_____

_____

CONCLUSION

Someone, probably a frustrated teacher, has proposed the following scenario: Jesus took his disciples up on the mountain and began to teach them: "Blessed are the poor in spirit, for theirs is the kingdom of heaven. Blessed are those who mourn, for they shall be comforted."

Then Simon Peter asked, "Do we have to write this down?" And Andrew said, "Will this be on a test?" And Philip said, "I don't have a pencil." And James said, "Do we have to turn this in?" And John said, "This is not fair. The other disciples don't have to learn this." And Judas said, "What does this have to do with real life?"

Then one of the Pharisees who was standing nearby said, "Where is your lesson plan and teaching outline of your main points? Where is your anticipatory set and learning objective in the cognitive domain?"

And Jesus wept.

Thank you for joining me in this brief time of praying through the beatitudes. If it was your first experience of praying scripture, I hope you will continue. Pick another portion of scripture, such as the Lord's prayer (Matthew 6:9-13), or one of Paul's letters, or perhaps a selection of Psalms.

If you are an experienced pray-er of scripture, I hope this book helped you build on what you had previously experienced, and thus strengthen your faith.

Now let me close with a scripture prayer for you:

The LORD bless you, and keep you;

The LORD make His face shine on you

And be gracious to you;

The LORD lift up His countenance on you,

And give you peace. (Numbers 6:24-26)

BEATITUDE BIBLIOGRAPHY

Allen, Charles L. *The Sermon on the Mount*. Westwood, NJ: Fleming H. Revell Co., 1966.

Allen, J. P. *The Sermon on the Mount: The Kingdom of God*. Nashville, Broadman Press, 1959.

Allen, R. Earl. *Divine Dividends*. Nashville: Thomas Nelson, 1974.

Allison, Dale C. Jr. *The Sermon on the Mount*. New York: Crossroad, 1999.

Augsburger, Myron S. *The Expanded Life*. Nashville: Abingdon Press, 1972.

Barclay, William. *The Beatitudes and The Lord's Prayer for Everyman*. New York: Harper and Row Publishers, 1963.

Boice, James M. *The Sermon on the Mount*. Grand Rapids: Zondervan Publishing House, 1972.

Carson, D. A. *The Sermon on the Mount*. Grand Rapids: Baker Book House, 1978.

Chambers, Oswald. *Studies in the Sermon on the Mount*. London: Marshall, Morgan & Scott, reprint, 1955.

Chappell, Clovis G. *The Sermon on the Mount*. Nashville: Cokesbury Press. 1930; Grand Rapids: Baker Book House, 1975.

Davis, William David. *The Sermon on the Mount*. Cambridge: University Press, 1966.

Eddleman,' H. Leo. *Teachings of Jesus in Matthew 5-7*. Nashville: Convention Press, 1955.

Fisher, Fred L. *The Sermon on the Mount*. Nashville: Broadman Press, 1976.

Graham, Billy. *The Secret of Happiness*. Garden City NY: Doubleday Inc., 1955.

Guelich, Robert A. *The Sermon on the Mount*. Dallas: Word Publishing, 1982.

Hankins Fred. *Earth's Greatest Sermon*. Orlando: Christ for the World, 1973.

Hargrove, H. H. *At the Master's Feet*. Nashville: Broadman Press, 1944.

Hastings, Robert J. *Take Heaven Now*. Nashville: Broadman Press, 1968.

Hendricks, Herman. *The Sermon on the Mount*. London: Geoffrey Chapman, 1979.

Henson, William E. *The Inaugural Message of the King*. New York: Vantage Press, 1954.

Hiemstra, Stephen W. *Life in Tension: Reflections on the Beatitudes*. Centreville, VA: T2Pneuma Publishers, 2016.

Howell, James C. *Beatitudes for Today*. Louisville, KY: Westminster John Know Press, 2006. :

Hunter, Archibald M. *A Pattern for Life*. Philadelphia: Westminster Press, 1953. Reprint 1965.

Kirby, Jeffrey. *Kingdom of Happiness: Living the Beatitudes in Everyday Life*. Gastonia, NC: Saint Benedict Press, 2017.

Jones, E. Stanley. *The Christ of the Mountain*. New York: Abingdon Press, 1931

Lloyd-Jones, D. Martyn. *Studies in the Sermon on the Mount*. Grand Rapids: Wm. B. Eerdmans Publishing Company, 1959.

MacArthur, John, Jr. *The Mac Arthur New Testament Commentary Matthew 1-7*. Winona Lakes, IN: BMH Books, 1985.

Meyers, F B. *Blessed Are Ye*. Grand Rapids: Baker Book House, 1955.

McEachern, Alton H. *From the Mountain*. Nashville: Broadman Press, 1983.

Montizambert, Eric. *The Flame of Life*. Greenwich, CT: Seabury Press, 1955. Paker,

Pentecost, J. Dwight. *Design for Living*. Chicago: Moody Press, 1975.

Pink Arthur, W. *An Exposition of the Sermon on the Mount*. Grand Rapids: Baker Book House, 1950, 1992.

Price, Nelson. *Supreme Happiness*. Nashville: Broadman Press, 1979.

Shinn, Roger Lincoln. *The Sermon on the Mount*. Philadelphia: United Church Press, 1962.

Stott, John R. W. *The Message of the Sermon on the Mount*. Downers Grove: Inter Varsity Press, 1978.

--------. *Sermon on the Mount: 13 Studies for Individuals or Groups*. Downers Grove: Inter Varsity Press, 1987.

Talbert, Charles H. *Reading the Sermon on the Mount: character Formation and ethical decision making in Matthew 5-7.* Grand Rapids, Michigan: Baker Academic, 2004.

Thompson, Ernest Trice. *The Sermon on the Mount.* Richmond: John Knox Press, 1946.

Tolar, William B. *Teaching Guide for Matthew 5-7.* Nashville: Convention Press, 1992.

Trench, Richard Chevevix. *Exposition of the Sermon on the Mount drawn from the Writings of St. Augustine.* London: MacMillian and Company, 1869.

West, Edward, N. *God's Image in Us.* New York: The World Publishing Company, 1960.

PRAYING SCRIPTURE BIBLIOGRAPHY

Boa, Kenneth. *Face to Face: Praying the Scriptures for Intimate Worship.* Grand Rapids, Michigan: Zondervan Publishing House, 1997.

Brueggemann, Walter. *Praying the Psalms: Engaging Scripture and the Life of the Spirit.* Eugene, Oregon: Cascade Books, 2007.

Campbell, Wesley and Stacey. *Praying the Bible.* Minneapolis, MN: Chosen Books, 2002, 2016.

Charis, Irene. *Praying the Scriptures: Reminding God of His Word in a Time of Need.* Meadville, PA: CreateSpace Independent Publishing Platform, 2016.

Cornwell, Judson. *Praying the Scriptures: A Field Guide for Your Spiritual Journey.* Lake Mary, Florida: Creation House, 1988,1998.

Hulderbrand, Lloyd. *Praying the Psalms Changes Things.* Alachua, Florida: Bridge-Logos, 2014.

Howard, Evan B. *Praying the Scriptures: Communicating with God in His Own Words.* Downers Grove, Illinois: InterVarsity Press, 1999.

Jackson, John Paul. *The Art of Praying the Scriptures: A Fresh Look at Lectio Divina.* Lewisville, Texas: Streams Ministries, 2016.

Merton, Thomas. *Praying the Psalms.* Collegeville, Minnesota: The Order of St. Benedict, 1956.

Moore, Beth. *Praying God's Word: Breaking Free from Spiritual Strongholds.* Nashville, Tennessee: B&H Publishing Group, 2009.

Prudhomme, Marty. *How to Pray and Never Run Out of Words: Praying the Scriptures.* Meadville, PA: CreateSpace Independent Publishing Platform, 2018.

Shepherd, J. Barrie. *Prayers from the Mount.* Philadelphia: The Westminster Press, 1986.

Shepherd, Linda Evans. *Praying God's Promises: The Life-Changing Power of Praying the Scriptures.* Ada, Michigan: Revell, 2018.

Stedman, Rick. *Praying the Psalms*. Eugene, Oregon: harvest House Publishers, 2016.

Towns, Elmer L. *Praying the Psalms: The Touch of God and Be Touched by Him*. Shippensburg, PA: Destiny Image Publishers, 2004.

_____. *Praying the Lord's Prayer for Spiritual Breakthrough*. Bloomington, MN: Bethany House Publishers, 1997.

_____. *Praying the Proverbs: Including Ecclesiastes & The Song of Solomon*. Shippensburg, PA: Destiny Image Publishers, 2005.

Whitney, Donald S. *Praying the Bible*. Wheaton, Illinois: Crossway, 2015.